MW00533603

Freedom & Prostitution

FREEDOM & PROSTITUTION

Cassandra Troyan

THE ELEPHANTS

Aileen Wuornos (February 29, 1956—October 9, 2002), was a sex worker usually referred to as the "first American female serial killer" after she was convicted of killing six men and sentenced to death for murder. Before her execution by lethal injection she refused to have an official public press conference. Instead she agreed to speak with Nick Broomfield, who was making his second documentary about her life, trial, and the media spectacle monetizing her death. It would be her last interview.

Nick Broomfield: But nonetheless.

Aileen Wuornos: Nobody ever asked me these questions.

N: Whether the cops were following you or not.

A: Whether the cops are following me or not, I mean what.

N: Okay, so let's say the cops were following you.

    A: Yeah.

N: Let's say they were following you and they did everything that you are saying they did.

    A: Uh huh. Yeah.

N: Nonetheless, you killed seven men.

    A: Yeah, I sure did.

N: And I am asking you what got you to kill the seven men.

    A: And I am telling you because the cops let me keep killing them Nick. Don't you get it?

N: Not everybody is killing seven people. So there must have been something in you that was getting you to do that.

    A: Oh, you are lost Nick!

N: So explain.

    A: I was a hitchhiking hooker.

N: Right.

    A: Running into trouble I'd shoot the guy if I ran into trouble, physical trouble, the cops knew it. When the physical trouble came along, let her – let her clean the streets. And then we will pull her in, that's why.

N: But how come there was so much physical trouble, because it was all in one year, seven people in one year.

    A: Oh well, oh well.

N: But why not say now.

    A: Because in retaliation for taking my life like this and getting rich off it all these years, in –

in total pathological lying. Yeah, thanks a lot. I lost my fucking life because of it. Couldn't even get a fair trial. Couldn't even get a fair investigation or nothing. Couldn't even have my appeals right.

You sabotaged my ass, society. And the cops, and the system, a raped woman got executed. It was used for books and movies and shit. Ladder climbs – re-elections and everything else; I got to put the finger in all your faces. Thanks a lot. You are inhumane. You're an inhumane bunch of fucking living bastards and bitches and you're gonna get your asses nuked in the end, and pretty soon it's coming. In 2019 a rock's supposed to hit you anyhow, you're all gonna get nuked.

You don't take fucking human life like this and just sabotage it and rip it apart like Jesus on the cross and say thanks a lot for all the fucking money I made off of you and not care about a human being, and the truth being told. Now I know what Jesus was going through.

I've been trying to tell the truth and I keep getting stepped on. Concerned about if I was raped, if I – I am not giving you book and movie info. I'm giving you info for investigations and stuff and that's it. We're going to have to cut this interview, Nick. I'm not going to go into any more detail. I'm leaving, I'm glad.

Thanks a lot society for railroading my ass.

For Aileen, Jami, Maya & Meg—

A flying stack   of cash
commands the air
its body   more material than yours
in the terrain   below
the poor   flagellating
themselves openly
in the fields
a secret misanthrope
vying for a tongue to share
lubricating this
arcane luxury
destitution is canny

How long have you been waiting for
the end
or for the light to return
your associations

With legs open to the window
you fuck the sun
you let it change you
you let yourselves be moved
to feel suddenly vibrant
in a space of inoculation
on another plane of recognition

Wherein the signifier of time fucks itself in the ass again and again and begs to come as what before seemed to be a relationship is now a difference in order.

When you asked him to speak his name, he told you about power instead.

When he told you not to tell anyone about us you assumed what he meant was the discourse of our relation.

When you tried to speak you realized you no longer had a tongue.

You were afraid of the signs because you already knew they meant a violence worse than death.

This violence on your body

You are told your symptoms prove
if she could only desire her freedom
then she'd be free

In the dream
        face was sunburnt
        presence   unchanging
  as was the landscape
  wringing out a slowness that predicts disaster

You only have one idea so you hold onto it
though in the dream
you are allowed more than one
        fantasy

In the dream
the soldier
moves
up and down
palms then elbows
then back again
     on the desert floor
in this heat
you open
not mysteriously
but by the weight
of a cold speculum
     dilating
     derailing
but not unpleasurable
evacuating   cavities
    a revelry of depletion
everything makes you wet
like after diagnosis
a declaration
     of war

He says how much
he loves you
that he will
never leave you
that you can never leave him
after he punches holes in the wall
    tears the door off its hinges
    throws you out of a moving car
    and tells you
    to find your way home

He comes back
    down the same country road
        he gets out of the car
        and crawls in the dirt
        crying at your feet
        begging for you to forgive him
        even though he says
        this is all your fault

In the dream you killed him
you were in a Walmart
he threatened you
he had a knife
to your throat
before he could finish
you moved him with
        your tears
    your arms around   his neck
    then just one
        choking him
    a telephone cord
around his throat
        you straddle him
        pinning   his arms
pulling the wire   taut
        he apologizes
        he does not struggle as his eyes go dim

You get up from his body
you know this is for the best
and wander the store
for several hours
       there is no egress
       only the vast horizon
       of ill compromise drying
       your tongue

You go to the service desk
    you are still crying
    as you look at   his dead body
    on the ground
    you were sure it would be gone by now
    you are about to tell the clerk
    at the counter about
               his body
    as you look on you see him move
    his limbs   stir freely
    as if only set in a   brief pause
    you are struck by a wave
    of mourning   and relief
    for his   undead body

    Will he still   know you
    since you have   killed him
    is your pact   made stronger
    will he ever forgive you
    will the next time be worse
    in this rift   of heated cruelty

Survival, an illness that perpetuates
the correlation and comforts
between the bed and the tomb
    like a framed golden Glock
     sheathed in the hull
        of your body

    To die tonight, to die in this bed—

The blade, the bed, or the sphere, which figure is
guilty of hypnosis is unclear.
You respond as if you understand your ineloquence.

He asks if you've ever been a working girl.
     You say you work
          every day of your life
          usually unpaid and when you are paid
          you're never really paid.

He says no, "a special friend," "a naughty girl," "a
secret girlfriend," "a playmate," "a dirty princess,"
"a friend with benefits," "a sensual lover," "Daddy's
girl," "Daddy's little girl," "Daddy's favorite girl," or
"a precious girl," but if you are a whore you can be
anyone.

You are a girl even though his children are your age

    His hands feel historical
    you, a football
    a tremble mass
    a girl on his shoulders

    The boys jeer at you
    Yes we love her cum-stained teeth
    Yes we love her droopy tits
    He covers you in beer
    he asks how much you love dick

He says you never put much effort into it, you
never put much effort into your crimes either.
You don't have much of a commodity out there.
You are overweight, you are beery, you never dress
as a prostitute, you never wear make-up, you
wear cut-offs, sneakers, a camo t-shirt, a cap and
glasses standing on the side of the road. He says if
you look at your hustle, you aren't soliciting. You
would get in the car and engage the situation…
you are running out of options.

If you are a prostitute of the twenty-first century
    metaphors are not enough
        delusions
        the girl who works
        who is she,
    always convincing
    convincing in capital
You are the whore on his yacht
    he asks you to shoot him up with heroin
    and you comply
    pay for all profitable demeanors
    which means disposability
        detracts your image from
        all the decorating cameras
    as "law does not ignore the bed"

To die tonight, to die in this bed—

The horror of the dead man's tongue in your mouth
pieces of his cheek flesh slough off in ribbons
    The participles   nut chunks like taste buds
        string cheese   always a cheese
        a most sour fermentation

The dead man loves how unbearable it is to open
your mouth to his
    How the decay comes rushing in
        gagging you
    He loves most that you must love it
    you are paid to love it in all its grotesqueness
    How good you are at that
    How you revel in your ability

        to eroticize abjection the greatest pleasures
        delivered from the sickest chores

How in thirty minutes he will cum on your chest
and this will all be over
as you are left in a luxury hotel suite
stack of cash on the bedside table
How the rest of the day is yours
and tomorrow
    and the day after that
    in your sudden freedom

How you make it rain
and roll around on the bed
the scent   of fresh currency
    as blue green gold reflects
    against your skin
       in the fading light

Or the days when it is too much
you are almost crying
you are holding back tears
as you fantasize about his death
    to get you through
    to get him off
    to get you off
and remember
that you can do almost anything
    for an hour

You are holding them back but you do not regret this
You do not want to be saved
You want the end of work not the end of sex
When one woman's death is another's survival

Fucking means nothing until you reside in its
absence, refuse its meaning, religiously

Scoring it, calcifying its lack
Get beaten for it
Drugged for it
Paid for it
Make a life of it

You hate no woman who has found herself
in the hustle
        discovered talent in the slime—
                dealing, stripping, fucking
                constantly redefining the bottom of
                everything

"Thus, I am leaving you to your own devices on
this bed. I am going out, and once again I will
write on the door so that, as you exit, you may
perhaps recall the dreams you will have pursued on
this bed."

Fantasies of harm and the form it gives to desire—
you question this. To drink from deleterious power
and ask *what can you make of me, this wreckage
of attachment?* Which pieces of your body reject
the rest of your body? How is your body in conflict
with your own politics? To stage a total revolt,
completely unimpressed with social barbarity

The body that eats its body
The body that protects the body
with a shimmering bark
The body that grows hooves now
The body that cries out
The body that refuses to die

You got cancer
You became sick
You killed yourself
You quit drinking
You became a hermit
You became a leper
You had both your breasts removed
You had your reproductive organs removed
You became homeless
You started using
You quit using
You declared bankruptcy
You turned to the streets
You became a prostitute
You became a student
You became a mother
You blamed yourself
You became a widow
You became an orphan
You became a criminal
You became a prisoner
You became a fantasy

Your body under the body of the dead man
You imagine he is a giant spider
    liquefying your vitality and sucking it from you

You tie him to the bed and tell him he can't touch you
       but you ride his face instead
         his moustache
         a spider you erase your cunt with
            scratching it out
            thrust by thrust
         in these moments when you love it
         for the love of fucking and
         for getting paid
         the lightness you feel
            in this unremorseful joy
            is the finest scam
            anyone can ever commit
            it is with this feeling
            that you go out into the night
            looking for a place to sleep
               for food   for a fix
            or the flying stack of cash
            he says flows from your pussy
            draining his bank account
                  and his cum

You laugh and in the background the chorus of sex workers calls out to say:

To fuck is to win / the joke's on him

When the dead man tells you meeting you is the best thing that has ever happened to him and he means it. The horror and tenderness you feel are not a contradiction but the culmination of a life's work.

"The presumption that she is a whore is a metaphysical presumption: a presumption that underlies the system of reality in which she lives. A whore cannot be raped, only used. A whore by nature cannot be forced to whore—only revealed through circumstance to be the whore she is."

She wants you to believe this. She keeps repeating herself as she tries to pull you from the lure of the chorus.

Every story is the same because it is not / you sought the cause and lost the plot

You took away a heft of generalities, yet you learned nothing, you broke nothing as your body ached transference. Your body released you from your hatred, your nature, your inability to complete the task both reaffirming and releasing in its pleasurable rejection as in the end, the joke's still on him.

"The whore has a nature that chooses prostitution.
She should be punished for her nature, which de-
termines her choice and which exists independent
of any social or economic necessity."

You believe women were made to be punished,
but there is no such thing as a woman—the limits
of violence created and held within this category,
woman.

The terror of being blamed for this violence, when
it goes beyond the typical "asking for it." When it is
a fetish, a proclivity, a pathological trait marked in
your nature. You cannot save a whore from herself,
you can only see that she recuperates and fulfills
the patterns graphed onto her.

The destruction of a body. A white body. A brown
body. A black body. A body reconstituting its own
glue, its own insatiable labors in a contract with
foes that holds you beyond choice. Afterwards
you discover your mistake, as you believed you
were a woman but you were actually the spider all
along—and in this—is a type of freedom.

And with your many legs, and fangs, and fantasies
of entrapment, and wetness, and poise, and voices,
and eyes, you go out with the chorus into the night
and cut the stillness with your laughter and fulfill
your practice—

When you call her a cab
When you draw her a bath
When you wipe away the blood
When you give her an alibi
When you let her sleep at your place
When you visit her in prison
When you pour her a drink
When you get her out of her house
When you teach her how to shoot a gun
When you bring her food in bed
When you keep her money for her
When you write her a letter
When you hold her close
When you walk her home
When you tell her she is not forgotten
When you say self-defense is not a crime
When you take her somewhere safe
When you clean out the minibar
on the dead man's tab

When you sit with the others and wait to repeat
Freedom means to win / Freedom, a life to claim and live again

It was like any other session. You had screened him and everything looked fine, you saw proof he was a union plumber. He called you when he got to the hotel lobby and you told him the room number. A few minutes later a knock on the door and you let him in. He knew to put the envelope on the table without you asking him and then he excused himself to use the restroom. To you he read as naturally submissive—eyes downcast, soft voice, a meek grin—when he came out of the bathroom though, something felt off.

You tell him to get on all fours and while your heel is planted on his shoulder he reaches and tries to grab you. You kick him on the side of his head, rolling him over onto his back, dropping a knee to his chest. He starts laughing.

You ask him what's funny as you slap his face and he reaches for his wallet and pulls out a badge and tells you you're under arrest. You say for what. He says prostitution. You say you're not a prostitute and he says you are now.

You laugh in his face, he hits you.
You spit in his face, he pulls out his gun.
He holds it to your head, you have no choice.
"Bitches like you die everyday."

When he raped you, you were not at work. While
he held you down and fucked you, you said "stop"
and "no" and used your safe word but he didn't
stop.

Afterward you felt numb.
You went to work the following day,
and then the next day.
And then the day after that, you think.
You can't remember.

When you finally talk to him about it he says he
doesn't remember, he calls you dramatic, he calls
you a liar, he calls you abusive.

You're in a BMW with a lawyer and he puts his
iguana tongue in your mouth and it tastes like
mothballs, martini, cheese, and you think you will
not survive this moment and then you do.

It happens, it has happened. It passes. You want
to cry, you are almost laughing and then you are
wet. The lawyer takes out a tit and flops it around.
He makes small wheezing noises as he rubs your
pussy outside your panties. He wants the man on
the street to see you. You feel shame not because
he is a man but because he is a laborer and you are
white and he is brown. He is going to the tortilla
factory where the other workers gather at four a.m.
and they roll open the metal door.

You remember this feeling that a second ago felt
so foreign even though you have encountered it
thousands of times. It is evasive, the dread lurching
up. What's the difference between this encounter
and another? What keeps the fear from you? What
keeps you alive? You feel no malice as you cum
hard with his fingers in your ass and you imagine a
giant stack of cash spilling out of your chest—you
take it up and toss it into the air.

The stack, instead of falling apart
    and slipping into singles
    takes flight
    the movement of paper wings
        gives rise
        to a sublime sensation
    of never having to think of money again
        flying into the horizon
        until it is a mirage
            a fable
            vanishing into history

You keep this fantasy close to you
It warms you when it is difficult to move forward
    When you worked the streets
        and hoped for the best
        because you didn't have
        any other options

        You learned in the Paris Metro
        that if you looked at men very directly
        they would follow you to buy a room
        this turned out to be much safer

In your attempts to survive
a client says
you're industrious and you say no

        Full   war
        for the sex workers against work

The chorus joins in:

Every time we fuck we are saying we will not punch a clock.
Every time we fuck our body belongs to us even if we're paid.
Every time we fuck we win.
Every time ends this garbage testimony that bleeds us—
> *The trick of every public face*
> *Every media image*
> *Every death, a statistic*
> *Every execution, a spectacle*
> *A list of names on a wall without faces*

> *Instead, the work of sabotage*
>> *Espionage*
>> *Every smile, a cover-up*
>> *Every kiss, in collusion*
>> *Every girlfriend, a sleeper*

We say tonight is a great night to refuse death in the veils
of power

You look at your face, the new version of your face
after you almost died. You still do not recognize
this face. Your mouth shaped differently by the loss
of so many teeth, the taste of your blood as you
hear him scream.

You do not remember the first blows.
He says, "That is my pussy, and I'm going to take it
back now."

You say you need help, that you need to go
to the hospital.
He says, "They can't help you," as he throws a dirty
blanket over you and you refuse to die.

Images of your brutalized body and face circle online. They are displayed so there can be no doubt left in anyone's minds, regardless if you deserved or provoked it, you are both victim and evidence of this violence. This is what the burden of proof requires—to be closest to the truth is to be almost dead.

To be brutalized
To be beaten
To be gagged
To be strangled
To be left for dead
To be assaulted
To be stabbed
To be raped
To be choked
To be drowned
To be poisoned
To be starved
To be tortured
To be enslaved
To be imprisoned
To be shamed
To be made hungry
To be sterilized
To be impoverished
To be kidnapped
To be erased
To be refused
To be hunted
To be murdered
To be eaten
To be skinned
To be dismembered
To be mutilated
To be buried
To be decapitated

You went around to ask everyone
if they heard of the girl found
in the lake with cinder blocks
                tied to her
                arms and legs
No one had
You think of this horror
how you could die in the same way
how no one would ever know
                or only
                a social phenomenon
                a small, familial tragedy
                to say their names

To say their names
    and refuse his
You don't want to say the soldier's name
you'll do anything to keep his name
    out of your mouth
        the name of every murderer
        a public fascination
    a site of obsession that reverberates
    louder than a memory of the dead
    "the Green River Killer" like a myth, a monster
        he said he killed you
        because God told him to
        he said you were evil
        you deserved to die
        he said you were easy to kill
        because everyone already
        expected you to die

Wendy Lee Coffield
Gisele Ann Lovvorn
Debra Lynn Bonner
Marcia Fay Chapman
Cynthia Jean Hinds
Opal Charmaine Mills
Terry Rene Milligan
Mary Bridget Meehan
Debra Lorraine Estes
Linda Jane Rule
Denise Darcel Bush
Shawnda Leea Summers
Shirley Marie Sherrill
Rebecca "Becky" Marrero
Colleen Renee Brockman
Sandra Denise Major
Alma Ann Smith
Delores LaVerne Williams
Gail Lynn Mathews
Andrea M. Childers
Sandra Kay Gabbert
Kimi-Kai Pitsor
Marie M. Malvar
Carol Ann Christensen
Martina Theresa Authorlee
Cheryl Lee Wims
Yvonne "Shelly" Antosh
Carrie Ann Rois
Constance Elizabeth Naon
Kelly Marie Ware

Tina Marie Thompson
April Dawn Buttram
Debbie May Abernathy
Tracy Ann Winston
Maureen Sue Feeney
Mary Sue Bello
Pammy Annette Avent
Delise Louise Plager
Kimberly L. Nelson
Lisa Yates
Mary Exzetta West
Cindy Anne Smith
Patricia Michelle Barczak
Roberta Joseph Hayes
Marta Reeves
Patricia Yellowrobe
Unidentified White Female (Jane Doe B-10)
Unidentified White Female (Jane Doe B-17)
Unidentified Female (Jane Doe B-20)

An aporia in time—
To be killed without the dignity of death
a void marked where death belongs
    bracketed by calculating
    the difference between
    disappearance and discovery

Deaths outside of time
    without a body
    or less than a body
    less than human
deaths only known by those who kill
    made a victim
    so they cannot be forgotten

The women known and unknown
To mourn the dead
To say more than their names

Wendy Lee Coffield, 16 disappeared July 8, 1982.

Your body was on found July 15, 1982. When they found you in the river your jeans were tied around your neck, strangling you. You were a dropout and runaway, you were often hitchhiking. Your mother said, "I know that was the kind of life she chose for herself, we taught her the best we could." Your mother said you were a good girl in the countryside and the trouble only began when you moved to the city, when she had to support you both. Sometimes you lived in a tent during the summer, you gathering blackberries to sell at the side of the road so you could buy food. In pictures, you had a wide smile spread across your open face.

Gisele Ann Lovvorn, 17, disappeared July 17, 1982.

Your body was found on September 25, 1982 near abandoned houses south of Sea-Tac airport. A pair of men's black socks were tightly tied around your neck. You grew up happy in California but started to run away when you were fourteen as you felt alone and isolated where you lived. You loved the Grateful Dead and followed them around the country to hear them play. You met your boyfriend on the road in Washington, he was a taxi driver and much older than you. You lived together in a small apartment and turned to street prostitution to bail him out of jail for theft. Your family didn't know what you were doing and were waiting for you to come home. You had long thick blonde hair and the bluest eyes.

Debra Lynn Bonner, 23, disappeared July 25, 1982.

Your body was found on August 12, 1982 floating in the river near the Kent slaughterhouse. Your mother Shirley sits at her kitchen table looking through photo albums filled with pictures from your childhood. Your mother said, "I love her with all my heart and I just wish to God she was alive and here." The last time she saw you was summer of 1982. "I couldn't believe it. I really couldn't believe it and it just seemed like it just seems like I was empty, like my whole body was empty." All your friends loved you, they said you were so beautiful. After you dropped out of high school you met your boyfriend who would later be your pimp. You traveled around, got arrested, lived in motels, but you still called your mother once or twice a week.

Marcia Fay Chapman, 31, disappeared August 1, 1982.

Your body was found on August 15, 1982. When you left the apartment, you told your three children you were going to the store and then never came back. Your mother said something like this had never happened. At 5' 2" and a hundred pounds your neighbors at the apartment complex called you "Tiny." Your neighbors described you "as cheerful, outgoing and someone who could take care of herself", "she was a nice girl." In the articles after your death none of them say that you are black. You had been arrested for prostitution two months before on the Pacific Highway South where you usually worked. You started at around five pm and would work through the night. You dressed casually, in a hat, jeans, and t-shirt. You never worked for a pimp, you said "why should I give the money to a man?... I need it for my kids, not for some man."

Cynthia Jean Hinds, 17, disappeared August 11, 1982.

Your body was found August 15, 1982 in the river by man who was collecting bottles and saw you held down under a pile of rocks. Your father, Robert, last saw you working as a cook at a South Seattle barbeque restaurant the day before you went missing. Your mother, Marilyn, said she knew you worked as a prostitute for three years after you got caught up with the wrong crowd and dropped out of Nathan Hale High School in North Seattle, although your father denied it. You sang in bars in King County and at community dances. After your death, your only recorded and original song, "Let's Fall In Love Again," was discovered and released by Fantasy Records in 1987.

You once told me love would last forever

You also said forever you'd be mine

We got something special

Don't let it slip away

'Cause love like ours is just too hard to find

Baby, (Oh baby) let's fall in love again

Like we did the first time

Baby, (Sweet baby) let's fall in love again

But this time never say goodbye

Your younger brother Terry said, "she still was a human being and she still had family that cared and loved her just like all the other ones had family that cared and loved them. And my sister she was a sweet person, a caring person and she was loved by a lot of people. After knowing she was dead, my life was just full of pain and my whole life just went down hill."

Mary Sue Bello, 25, disappeared October 11, 1983.

Your remains were found Oct. 12, 1984. Growing up you believed your mother was your older sister, and your grandparents were your parents. Your mother was only fifteen when she had you. When you found out you never forgave her for lying to you. She thought it would be better to raise you like this, instead of giving you up for adoption. Your mother had been adopted. When she found out she was adopted, she never forgave her parents for hiding it from her. They said they wanted to protect her from the horrific details of her past. Her birth mother left her siblings alone and her brother died in a fire, but her twin sister survived. Her birth parents divorced and her birth mother went to Alaska and left her in a boarding house alone. It was three days until they found her, she was only six months old. You wanted to know where your father was, who he was. When you finally met your father after he got out of prison, he tried to rape you. You realized then you never had a father. Your mother pleaded with you to stop prostituting yourself, but you insisted, this was the way you had to make money, you had no other options. The last time your mother saw you she said she had a feeling of dread as you she saw you leave your trailer for the bus stop. She said, "the punishment for prostitution should not be death."

Opal Charmaine Mills, 16, disappeared August 12, 1982.

Your body was found August 15, 1982. Chubby cheeks, sweet girl, innocent, strong-willed, kind, charismatic. How many deaths do these women die, what does it mean if you died loved, if you died cherished. If your family mourned your loss, if your father drank himself to death. It's a kind of terror to repeat these fragments, the residue of a life that circles around itself. The violence of your father's rage—how he'd beat your brother, lock the cabinets and refrigerator because he thought you both ate too much, the refrigerator covered with drawings commanding you to be thin, to have a flat stomach. To be abandoned by your family, when they give up because their family gave up on them. Generations of trauma. You were named after your father's sister who was murdered in Oakland. He never stopped blaming himself, and your brother never stopped blaming himself for your death.

Debra Lorraine Estes, 15, disappeared September 20, 1982.

Your body was found May 30, 1988. Then to die with you, to die in this ditch, to die strangled in the woods, is not histrionics it is embodied mourning that marks each of you as singular even in your similarities, in your joy and pain. What it means to travel alone, to turn to a life on the streets. What it means to be white and pretty. What it means to be black and pretty but have less options, less sympathy from the cops, from pimps, from johns, from murderers. What it means when your life is worth less. What it means for your mother to leave your abusive father, to move from man to man to man when she cannot earn enough on her own. What it means when you don't trust men but depend on them to live. What it means when your boyfriend pimps you out, when you think this is love. What it means when no one can protect you, when no one can save you but yourself.

Mary Bridget Meehan, 18, disappeared September 15, 1982.

Your body wasn't found until November 13, 1983 in a shallow grave a few blocks from the Red Lion Motel. You were eight months pregnant. Brilliant young woman, so intelligent and sensitive, a genius, they said. Try to understand what went wrong. To be abandoned by your family, thrown out, the door locked and your key no longer works. They beg you to come home but only on their terms. You had two miscarriages as a young teen. You think about your life as a distant dream, to speak only about what you could never do, to let the impossibility of the future be what makes you believe in life but what also keeps you from it. Victim of the times, of drugs, of too much dreaming, they said. Your life is not separate from your death. *It could have been you, it is you.* Your death is not a tragic spectacle. It is a reality. You die together.

Linda Jane Rule, 16, disappeared September 26, 1982.

Your remains were found January 31, 1983. Remains, not a body. The difference between what makes up a body and what is not enough to make a body. The media called it "a dump site," the police called it a "body site." The fragments of you at a body site, mixing with the evidence of a crime. "fibers, hair, rocks, paint chips, twigs, loose finger and toenails, bits of bone, rotted pieces of cloth, fragments of cheap jewelry, tiny slips of paper, a cigarette, photos and moulages of tire tracks, a condom." *Your blonde hair, your smile, your rosy cheeks, your tear-stained cheeks, your blue eyes, your green eyes, your brown eyes, your tired eyes, your crying eyes, your buxom chest, your willowy limbs, your petite frame.* Only a collection of bones in a ditch next to the highway is found. He didn't bother to dig a grave. As the seasons go by, your body builds its own grave, sinking deeper into the ground as the earth covers you. To die tonight—to die in this bed.

As you repeat these names
        you know it is not enough
        memory is not enough
To mourn your dead
To say the names
You continue
with every trick turned, a triumph
in recognition and refusal
        to die alone
                in your bed
                in your streets
Yet to know that you will be punished
        for your survival
To be killed for your own defense
as a prostitute is either redeemed
murdered or murders
        Criminal, victim, or hero—
        who is the monster now?

It is no mistake that Aileen Wuornos had to die. Insane, sexually abused, abandoned, raped, crude, traumatized, a dyke, ugly, unhinged, mentally unsound, debased by incest and poverty. Your life and your death, a spectacle to be consumed. After your death a beautiful actress performs a caricature of you. They praise her for how ugly she has become, they call it art and give her an award.

Charlize Theron: "No, I had to get to a place of understanding. When I was playing her, I always used to say to Patty, 'God, if only she didn't do this one thing. How would her life have turned out?' It's a very emotional place to be. I read the story and immediately related and responded to that. That wasn't tough for me. It wasn't like I was reading this very distant thing that I couldn't understand at all. She was a normal human being that had gone through a lot of heartache. I related to that on a different level. I think you have to get to a place where the best you can do is understand—maybe—why, and then really drag yourself through it, because it's tough to do those things. The last killing, it was impossible. It was one of the worst nights of my life…We all might go through rough spots in our lives. [But for her] there was never a break, and half of it is not even in the movie because you just don't have enough time. The fact is there are so many times that she really did try to change her life. That was the one thing that I really loved about her—that she wasn't the kind of person who sat back and went, 'Well, I'm a prostitute and this is my life.' She tried to join the army! And they wouldn't take her because she was deaf in one ear, because she had been beaten so badly."

Before they executed you said, "I'll be back, I'll be back."

You don't leave the bed

You don't go
        you don't take
        for granted
you try to come to terms with your suffering as
        punishment and tool against you
        you take the heart out
        you try to leave
        you take up a passage
        you try to test the value
        you fail through the force of fallow vision
        you're told it's all your fault
        you don't know the stakes

        your stupidity
        your exhaustion
            working   wilting
            you writhe this one out

A flying stack of cash
     breeding fantasies of
     freedom and domination
     the guilt allayed
in this seduction   the cause
and response of your femininity
You feel stupid, you're to blame
     the kinds of games women
persecute themselves with
the kinds of scenes they
              cannot leave

From the bed you can see him
    desert tan tactical boots
    his hair stiff with dust
    a skull stretched across his face
    flying at 120 knots   a door gunner
    with a M-240H machine gun
        on a UH-60 helicopter
        scanning the landscape
        at 50 to 5,000 feet
    the village is a plane of coordinates
    navigable through erasure

The sequence is maligned
a child bends out the window
a glass is slipped across the table
and you are caught
in this familiar architecture
a colonial romance

    A fake heartbreak that leads
    to a real heart
the limits of genuine risk
and the bodies you will
    hold close
    on fractured overpasses
    and broken buildings

Traditions of violence
ricochet
from your body
to the images of every village
every bedroom
he took from behind a gun
a first glimpse of seduction
in the courting
you become closer
      unimaginable
          every time you look at him
you think of everyone
he's killed
long beard   his clothes
         how easily he passes
         without a uniform
         the ways of a traitor
an imperial position
calling this chimera
chest coated in cash
         making it rain
         counting down the nights
         at the club
until you can finally leave him

Every soldier, a john
Every husband, a dead man

This world must disappear without
        tragedy or irony
        fantasy not a threat
                but a conceptualizing force
        that builds the possibility of wrecking
        for and against itself

Like the flight of a helicopter
levity   a contradiction
                in form

You try to destroy the bed
   but the grave
   still a better promise
   when the struggle is
      daily life
   every act of resistance
      homed in monuments
      crystals
   fallen to minerals
      a current
      of dishonesty
      unrecognizable
   shredded down
   questioned down
   to the practice of forever
   between
   the margins

What it means
        to reside there
        survive there
        attempt to thrive
        in an impossible history
        where death
        is the softest alcove
        and love the imminent heart
        of a heartless world
            or is that what makes it transgressive

The dead man is not finished with you yet
you could see him before he even arrived.

He comes back after his first deployment and
goes to your parents' house to look for you but
you were already gone.
Your sister answered the door to say you didn't
live there anymore.

Euthanasia
a solitude
meditating at a bay-window
holding a shit-varnished template
    placate the skin
    tear back the flesh
    into a gender of mourning

You wish you could never see him again
You wish he had never found you

Crying on a platform
like it's mid-century
you've got a handkerchief to prove
    nothing gets better with time
    your hands are still freezing
    you've killed yourself
    a thousand times in this city
you've prayed without sound
    you couldn't believe
    when you opened your eyes
        your hands at your chest
        the reluctance of loneliness
catastrophe without break
no angels in the hallway
no messianic luxury

You walk up a gilded staircase surrounded by a
thousand mirrors
       no reflection   all wreckage and warnings
       "bitches get what they deserve"

You go to a room and the soldier opens the door,
he lets you in he kisses you and asks why you've
kept him waiting. He doesn't wait for an answer.
He grabs you, undresses you as he pulls you to the
bathroom.

       You struggle but he squeezes your throat
       lifts you up against the wall by your neck.
       The room goes black as he tightens his grip.

    You don't remember where you are
    or how long you've been out.
    You wake up to him standing above you,
    pissing on you.
    Smiling, he looks down and says
    good morning sweetheart

You ask him if you're going to die
he says
I'm going backwards in time
lifting at three am
watching the sun come up
        waiting for when
        we meet again
        on the other side of war

Death reopens a channel to the past
he says,
when you almost die
you don't cry for humanity
or yourself
no grievances
no tears
candle wax melodies
playing in the background

He says
a real man   is
the terror in the landscape
     both local and sublime
He says he's come across
so many mass graves
     a dozen here
     a dozen there
but there is no measurement for the cruelty
of a terrain

He says *even in a civil war*
     there are many sides

He drags you by your hair
from the bathroom to the bedroom
    you scream
he kicks you and tells you not to resist
he throws you on the bed
he climbs on top of you
    he says, *I don't want to fuck you just yet*

He starts to choke you again
the weight of his body pressing you down
    into the bed
    he throws a pillow on your face
    he starts to smother you
    under this pressure you begin to cry
    your sobbing shakes your whole body
    until his fucking takes over
    and you wait for him to finish
    leaving you relieved and shivering

He picks you up
He holds you and tells you not to cry

To die tonight, to die in this bed—

The cruelty of compulsion
        you think you might puke
in your attempt to find a language without
boundaries
        you're speaking like any other dead girl
        waiting for the sunset
        a small spiritual contract
        in this coercive forever
you looked for slight entrances
but were never relieved
            the force of biology
            and amorous terror
            you ask
                what kills a man
                what breaks him

Abolish this encounter
marking you as
disposable
instead your resilience
a threat
    God   guns   goals in the
face of immanent cause
reflecting this   sensitive beauty
    a human diction
holding you up by the chest
until your tits rip off
and you're never forced to be
    a woman again

He called the summer a vision
a fulfillment of orders
the men kept returning to the house
each time they would drive up to it
    a shade of fog
    grew belly first
    crowded in
the driveway
relapsing
    a ceaseless diversion

You make the necessary arrangements
    set the signals
    the details
    decoys and wait

You refuse the dream but it returns to you
there are only singularities
clinging with a volatile touch
the scene of his appearance
revealed
an obsession with recognition
recoiling
for affirmation
a kiss
a night alone in a house
in a field
all that land
to be lost to

In bed you wake up in his arms
>and roll over to slit his throat
>and watch as the blood soaks the sheets

>To die tonight, to die in this bed—

A real man
There is only one
    and for him
    that is the only light
        left to bear
To create what breaks you
    when you left the bed
    took all his guns
    burned down his house
    and he never had to be
        a man again

But you are like most women
    unafraid of the truth
when every night an insect is your father
the entire world an electrical current
strange how it's only a glimpse
    the weight of holding all the rage
    that no one else can be bothered to carry

A civic duty
this work of love
to be abased by
the particularities of refusal
the kindness of its loss
and your freedom in its destruction

The chorus arrives and you are
on the move again no longer afraid

When the world is an illusion
constructed by the state
a diabolical resolution
    you cannot believe that
    the war will be over soon
To surrender to
an ideology of hunger
    to walk down the street
    and not feel shame
strength in the fortune plea—
You can't do that to me anymore
I'm not afraid of you
    To want to be something other than
    your life now

But to wait for the end that
          never comes
          never disintegrates
lesser methods of choosing
peace over retribution
               silence over pain
          when your survival
          is the greatest revenge

Dividends   disasters and other
unraging signs of your over-determination
    your inability to see a variety of signs
    patterns calling out our errors
to only recognize figures
you are told are like your own
to see yourself
    in the distance
    a subject
    presented untroubled
    a closure that stops you
    before you begin

Until inexplicably
the world opens again

In the dream there is an arena
the crowd pours in
an exhaustion ripping past
all injuries
    dressing   perilous reportage
there is only one voice
    no excuses
    no attempts to push back
    this stupid   swallowing
    weapons   being distributed
    hand-made and stolen
blood soaks   the AstroTurf
below is the earth
and   is split open
but   is down there
and you on   the hillside
    patrolling through
weeds   marshes   trenches
    knee-deep in a
    clotted muck

when you look down   you see
    the mud is clotting
you try to run but
    fouled blood stops you
below is the earth
your teeth
    are bleeding but
below is the earth
below is the earth
    in the night
the night your death was glorious
the night you looked into the mirror
cut lines into faces against your parents
the night you couldn't fake it anymore
against appropriation
against decorous resolution

Poet laureate of the insurrection
communiqué
against a tie man pressing boobies
cutting flesh taking water source
flushing tactile
police batons erotic tenderizers
synthesize ethics of
chewed up love laws
from the food bank to robbing banks
take this unchurned bomb and
set it free
paint the walls with your blood
violence is not what you do
it is the betrayal you depart from
a nightshade talisman
calling in your debts

This is what you call gratitude
and all coarse affections
      pantomiming your deaths
Do you want more or do you take more?
This isn't destiny or
      some higher resolution
the smell of an orchard   after dawn
a pastoral deflection
      you can't let yourself recognize
like the pavilions you've backed into
      through the labor of time
      the machines on your back
      mirroring   every symbolic
         scene of progress
         your abjection

The whip   the cross   the field   the bed
          form greater bonds
     by what they deny   not extend
     in tokens of discipline
               blasphemy   terror   remorse
          and grief for all difference unnamed

Tarring & Feathering
Drawing & Quartering
Water-boarding
Electrocution
Poisoning
Decapitation
Disembowelment
Lethal Injection
Firing Squad
Torturing
Hanging
Suffocation
Strangulation
Flagellation
Asphyxiation
Drowning
Crucifixion
Burning
Branding
Garroting
Gibbeting

Impaling
Pendulum
Sawing
Scaphism
Starvation
Stoning
Boiling
Castration
Combing
Crushing
Flaying
Sawing
Scalping
Torturing by rats
Devouring by animals
Trampling by horses
Crushing by elephants
Blowing from a gun
Breaking wheel
Burying alive

The individual tortured body
and the collective tortured body
The future is removal
and a new orifice for every body
every body an orifice
every body a hole of disconsolation

A transition is a war
at the center of loneliness
    that fear cannot hold
    to ask what is your greatest forgiveness
       the unjustifiable cause that suffers
         this separation
    exhaustion at every hour of the day
      a different prose

Which world was this? The frame or its erasure?
When all attachments feel lethal
this dull opulence is a cold seduction of remission

The old world and its codes
    its blood sighs and its fractures
        accentuating this aberration
        called home
    you knew you could make a new one
        and be better

The materiality of this world.

You could not describe its objects but the processes are now more palpable, articulated with seductive clarity.

A sensuality. A voluptuous congress accentuating every tongue. When everything you do is public, with no life to go to after the day—no togetherness postponed, a temporary in situ for the shuddering forms of a body in practice.

You travel mostly at night or at dawn
sometimes in groups of 200 or more
through the underbrush, through sewers and forests
and garbage and ditches
close to the ground where it is difficult
to move   but small enough
to be protected by   the rough chaparral
or barbed wire
lookouts circling overhead

Dramatic feeding
with buoyancy and grace
extirpation
how did you   imagine
to be any different
on the executioner's block
every whore gets what she is asking for

You are carried
until you learn to walk again
bringing your mother animals
and placing them in her mouth
surrounding her with flowers
    not funereal
but to feed   this enclosure
    she cannot leave
"the tender and innocent heart
    of all systems of power"
    find new comforts
    outside the symbolic

You try to drink
but the glass of water is almost too large
and too heavy to reach your mouth
    you lift it quickly
so you can hold it before it slips
    from your grip
while trying not to spill
or smash the glass

This is the fantasy of opposites—
    how to live in the world
    with those you don't trust

You forgot how to write
the pen keeps falling out of your hand
        or your grip is too strong
        and it snaps the pen in two
    or your script is so sharp
    you rip the page and by the time
you're finished there is no page left

This is a theory of antagonism—
how to have the same conversation for the next
    ten, twenty, two hundred years
how to be the only one to say
    we've been here before
    in a meaningful way

You wake up and someone else is dead
    you saw your sister die
    you saw your mother die
    when you say goodbye
    it makes death real

    Walking down the street
        lights up
        it's midnight
        no cars   no rain
            no tears

You blinked again and again
but you couldn't clear   your vision
you were separated from the others
        you called out shrilly
        and were answered

        You slip away while
                enemies argue
                amongst themselves
                "ghosts of the plains"
        stabbing at internal organs
        or chasing down on foot

A telephone rings
You answer it and a woman's voice tells you
>   *"I can't leave if I don't break*
>   *with the enemies that I've*
>   *unmasked"*

You hang up the phone and walk across the street
to a boarded up liquor store
>   above it is an apartment building
>   with blown out windows
>   >   you climb the fire escape ladder
>   >   to the top floor and crawl inside
>   >   >   to shed your fear

The room is full of women
    some from the chorus
    some from old families
      the street
      other cities
You open your mouths to each other
        sloshing a venom
           trickling in
You say the erotic is a kind
of undeniable present and
you can't wait any longer
you untie all the shoes
you lick every sole
you make yourself available
    and open
you talk and laugh
planning   discussing
some in a corner of the room
    fucking   in the sun
      but not separate
as they add to the conversation

This is the reality of participation—
how to be separate but not a spectacle
how to be included but not a spectacle of appearance

You feel the threat of narrative
the weight of   bodies
the not   that holds your
        ecstatic refusal
    held by a stress   unbearable
an anxiety produced   in waiting
resonant querulous reports
    small family groups
    scuttling   soft vocalization
        WHERE are YOU?

Predatory and potent
erotic assimilations
     stack in the sky
     feeding in the air
     watching the forests below
others are nearby at different levels of interaction—
sometimes enemies   sometimes friends or
                                        both

     You call out
     in love or distress
     sounds resemble the cities
     that used to exist
     the names of the dead
     how to articulate
          this history that will be
          through the past undone

Dramatically   you strike
from the sky
and no longer fear repression
generally quiet
remain undetected until your shadows
        flood the water
until you are overcome
with this feeling of
when you were
the most alone
revenge rises up in the back
of your throat
entices dissimilarities
        in the dark
unloved
obliterate the signal
to no longer refuse the truth
because of its power to destroy
        like any good hunter
        a disrespectful scavenger
        a thief suspended in prolonged soaring

Bodies become one body
sinks down to a radical emptiness
        you learn configurations
        use your force with others
                in a skillful balance
            of resistance and capture
                how to destabilize
                you never put it to use
                against each other
                to hold   a tender
                suspension of violence
                compelling meaning
                this is your training your resilience

You place your body
        on other bodies
    they are full of erotic potential
    redirected rather than ignored
How to build without producing
        each day   another set of obstacles
    linked into commonality
    a pleasure shared
        to never be alone again
        to cross it all out

One by one records of actions compile into another larger body, a tactile expanding body that communicates beyond and without and in this unwieldy shifting mass, a joy not unlike revenge, fills you with possibility. You continue to work, not out of habit, but to take up this joy from within, an immersive tactic.

Passing coins of spit
    the sex of exchange
    that aligns you
in this otherwise random coupling
a momentary release   sugar slip

He tells you to get up off the bed
and undress more slowly this time
while looking at him in the eyes

You bend over
    and the world's upside down
    your ass in the sun
    your ass is the sun
    a currency of light
that refracts at the last moment
    and you watch his face
    unfold as he comes
    and it drips to the floor

You pick up his face
    and try it on
    sticky sensations turn to
    a formal and pleasing
        response
    and you open his mouth
        to breathe in your air
        to win against the memory of
    that one time you almost died
           in the Trump Hotel
    as a man was laughing laughing
        laughing above you
        and you could feel yourself
        fading until
        there is a faint scratching
        coming from outside
        bristling   millions of follicles
    crumbling   the world slowly eating itself
    hooves scales   cut the shell tear the sac
           hooks dragging
    rotten eggs   rotten eggs
    and you know the chorus
        is on their way

You create a ceremony
you sit in a room facing forward
making small sounds
since you cannot look at anyone
          you are permitted to cry
weeping bodies make a rustling that begins
slowly gaining in heat and friction
     the entire building vibrating
          shifting in   landscapes
          territories   continents
               until the dead are here

This is not a fantasy
    you are in the room with the dead
    you raise the dead
    from the deserts
    from the mass graves
    from the shallow graves
    from the oceans
    from the rivers
    from the lakes
    from the sewers
    from the city dumps
    from the forests
    from the ditches

"Out of the grave
    and into the streets!"

You gather with tens of thousands, hundreds of thousands, you lose count as they try to smash you all smear you against glass ground you into the street you move your broken limbs and continue on as your individual body is unheroic, unassuming as you begin to move across the city like a smear.

This goes on for a long time. You limp around, you dig a burrow for the earth to surround you, you regenerate, you wander at night looking for others. You create diversions, traps, tripwires for intruders. You share food.

You are on different continents yet this doesn't matter since you are now so many you can bridge across them. You go to the capital to show one of your arms that was found at a dumpsite with some of the flesh removed. You weep, you sing, you chant in unison, and you rain curses on all the killers.

You start to speak and the crowd goes silent. *"Any ritual killer, who attempts to take life will be punished … If he thinks … a prostitute has no worth … make sure he does not live to tell his own story. You say it now and confirm it, that as far as you are concerned … you babes are ready for them. They should come with their charms. You will deal with them. Now, you are potent as a bomb."*

You have heard the last gurglings of power
    indebted to an order of sun
    a cracking pelvis   a shattering jaw
      a palace burns
    You stand silent
    You start again

You must be terrified of this life until you destroy it.
The whore must believe in revenge.

    Let's look at this crowbar, what do you see?
      You call it a process
      You call it freedom
      You call it deflecting
      You call it a bouquet of errors

Instead of running, now you hunt. You remember you are the spider.

You have taken over a local TV station and in place of a news anchor you talk of your plans and command the frame.

"You'll get him first, yeah, you are going to get him first. When you find him, he is going to be sorry. It is as simple as that."

Resistance
how does it devastate
        and mark you
no more healing as justice
no more vigils or candlelit sympathy
no more compromises
        to steal away a cyclical motion
                of harm
How you'd wear the night
on your chest
all the beauty in your refusal
your bravery pushing through
thought you couldn't go on
        a feather of the time you spoke
        while you cut the world in stars
and said it's not the end
                to not relinquish
                to not retreat

Remember how he said he liked
to keep your bodies in groups that he called clusters
he would drive by
and think of the women placed there
of others he'd like to add

Bodies
now a social accumulation asking
what revives what kills
The collection of
    your skin peeling away in thick slabs
    your limbs falling off
    your remains
    your bones
    your smiles
    your tears
    all the parts slipping
        into a pile
        a spilling architecture
    cracking   as it grows
until it forms chains of tensile structures
    growing and shrinking
    through teething
    and molting
    a new breathing

Notes

Whether militaristic, imperialistic, or carceral, the violence women face in sex work or their intimate relationships are intrinsically linked by the force of capitalism and its capacity to shape and impoverish everyday life. This work is in solidarity with the struggles of sex workers everywhere. This book would mean nothing without the stories and lives of all women, along with genderqueer, non-binary and gender non-conforming people who have experienced gendered violence and their courage to overcome and live. This is in dedication to survivors everywhere, for every sex worker who refused to die a statistic, and in remembrance for those lost, though remembrance is never enough.

Candlelight vigils do not avenge the dead. Different forms of recognition or justice have deeply informed and shaped my own experiences of violence and resilience as a survivor. My political position doesn't stop at visibility, but the necessity for the abolition of work in of itself. From this, a truly libratory politics can begin.

Sex work is not a "better" type of labor, but a proposal for the abolition of all labor. In *Freedom & Prostitution*, freedom means liberation and autonomy – a world without work, without money, without gender – and imagines forms of survival now for those who have few if any choices, refuse to submit to the demands of tedious underpaid or unwaged labor, an abusive partner, and/or seek a life beyond work.

It is a text indebted to what is left behind—at a crime scene, a home, a back alley, a hotel room, a squat, or a riot. <u>Citation,</u> which is always a world-building and political act, requires direct recognition when necessary, or anonymity to protect the criminal underclass. Through fragments, notes, overheard conversations, and traces of disappearance, the following acknowledgements indicate the ways resilience and power shape knowledge and identification (or the lack thereof).

༄

From sex workers who tell their stories of intimate partner violence but are less likely to be believed because they're sex workers, such as with Christy Mack and Stoya, to the figure of Aileen Wuornos who is treated as both a victim and criminal because she sought self-preservation. The documentaries *The Life and Death of a Serial Killer* (2003) and *The Selling of a Serial Killer* (1992) both by Nick Broomfield help depict a complex image of Aileen Wuornos. The interview with Charlize Theron in 2004 examines her depiction of Aileen Wuornos in *Monster* (2003). In the introduction, interviewer Carlo Cavagna of AboutFilm.com described Theron as "Best known for her stunning beauty, the statuesque twenty-eight year old South African native achieves a remarkable transformation in Monster. To portray notorious Florida prostitute/serial killer Aileen Wuornos, executed for seven murders in 2002, Theron gained weight and subjected herself to an unflattering makeover—both physical and emotional." Much of the discussion of Theron's Academy Award Winning performance refers to this transformation.

"You are the whore on his yacht / he asks you to shoot him up with heroin / and you comply" is in reference to a case from 2013, where Alix Tichelman, a sex worker in Santa Cruz, CA met a client, named Forrest Hayes, a Google X executive, on his yacht. During the evening, he asked for her to inject him with heroin, later leading to his death by cardiac arrest. In the media, she was portrayed as a violent coldblooded killer since she left him passed out without calling an ambulance, though she was already a criminal regardless of her actions.

The aphorism "law does not ignore the bed" is Jacques Lacan's – On Feminine Sexuality, The Limits of Love and Knowledge: Encore 1972–1973 (1999) – as is the excerpt "thus, I am leaving you to your own devices on this bed. I am going out, and once again I will write on the door so that, as you exit, you may perhaps recall the dreams you will have pursued on this bed."

The echoes of "Every time we fuck we win" from the sex worker chorus is from Ingrid Ryberg's text of the same title "Every time we fuck we win: The public sphere of queer, feminist and lesbian porn as a (safe) space for sexual empowerment" in *The feminist porn book: the politics of producing pleasure* edited by Tristan Taormino, Celine Parreñas Shimizu, Constance Penley, Mireille Miller-Young (2013).

Excerpts on "the whore's nature," from Andrea Dworkin's *Pornography: Men Possessing Women* (1979) articulate ways whorephobia and stigma are reproduced in spaces and by people one would hope would be first in solidarity with sex workers.

In the actions by the chorus there are references to sex workers and women who are survivors of assault or domestic violence, yet were punished for their acts of self-defense, especially because they are African-American. In August 2010, Marissa Alexander fired a warning shot towards her estranged husband who was threatening to kill her. Even though Florida has stand-your-ground laws, making such an act legal, she was sentenced the mandatory minimum of twenty years in prison for aggravated assault. She continued to fight her case, serving only three years, and is now free and speaks publically on the criminalization of survivors. In August 2014, Cynthoia Brown, a sixteen year-old homeless runaway engaging in survival sex, killed client Johnny Michael Allen in his home as an act of self-defense when she thought he was reaching for his gun. Despite being a minor, she was tried as an adult and sentenced to 51-years-to-life in prison.

In 2017 national media campaigns by celebrities drew attention to her case calling for Tennessee Governor Bill Haslam to grant Brown clemency, claiming she should be seen as a victim of poverty, a pimped out "sex slave," who was "sex trafficked," though during her trial she was referred to as a "teen prostitute." (Brown came to understand herself as a victim of trafficking but never as a "sex slave.") She spent fifteen years behind bars until she was released on August 7, 2019.

In 2015 porn performer Stoya publically spoke about her rape by her then-boyfriend and scene partner, James Deen. This opened a space for other women to come forward to talk about violence they experienced while shooting scenes with him, as well as interpersonal and domestic violence.

In 2014 former porn performer Christy Mack was brutally beaten and sexually assaulted by her ex-boyfriend and former MMA fighter "War Machine," in what she truly believed was an attempt to kill her if she hadn't escaped. During the attack War Machine said, "now I have to kill you. I've gone too far."

Ann Rule's *Green River, Running Red: The Real Story of the Green River Killer—America's Deadliest Serial Murderer* (2005) provides a basis for the narratives of these women's lives, with references to journalistic sources that speak to families and friends in trying to make sense of these horrible events. In remembrance of these women, Annie Sprinkle and other sex workers at SWOP (Sex Worker

Outreach Project) turned December 17 into a day for mourning the deaths of the victims of the "Green River Killer" and other victims.

The phrase "bitches get what they deserve" are from the songs "SUFFER FOREVER" and "All Bitches Die (All Bitches Die Here)" by the artist and musician Lingua Ignota, a.k.a. Kristin Hayter.

"The tender and innocent heart of all systems of power" and "I can't leave if I don't break with the enemies that I've unmasked" come from Tiqqun's "Sonogram of a Potential" (2002).

"Passing coins of spit the sex of exchange" was inspired by Rona Lorimer's "Eliza in Autumn."

"Out of the grave and into the streets!" is a reference to Anne Boyer's "What Resembles the Grave but Isn't."

The story of resistance told by Nigerian sex workers who marched on the Nigerian Union of Journalists's headquarters in 2015 to protest and avenge the death of their friend, Sitira, 25, of Abeokuta in the state of Ogum, Nigeria.

These powerful words are from friend and sex worker Tee-Baby: "Any ritual killer, who attempts to take life will be punished…If he thinks…a prostitute has no worth…make sure he does not live to tell his own story. You say it now and confirm it, that as far as you are concerned…you babes are ready for them. They should come with their charms. You will deal with them. Now, you are potent as a bomb."

Acknowledgements

Excerpts of this manuscript have been published in the following publications:

An excerpt entitled, "This World Must Disappear," was published in *Elderly*, Issue 9: Too Big to Fail, April 2015, thanks to editors Jamie Townsend & Nicholas DeBoer.

"POSTSCRIPT FOR A FUTURE'S PAST," was published in *Armed Cell: Post-Crisis Poetics*, April 2017 and "This World Must Disappear," was published in *Armed Cell 10*, April 2016, thanks to editor Brian Ang.

An excerpt entitled, "What Remains," was published in *Tripwire 14: The Red Issue*, May 2018, thanks to editor David Buuck for publishing it.

Marie Buck published an excerpt from *Freedom & Prostitution*, on *Social Text Online* on August 8, 2019. I'd like to extend special thanks to Marie for her close attention to the very tedious formatting of the piece.

An excerpt from *Freedom & Prostitution* was published in *Partial Zine 2* in August 2019, thanks to editor Adam Katz.

Thank you to Tom Allen for including an excerpt of *Freedom & Prostitution* in the one-off publication published in August 2019, *We do not believe in the good faith of the victors* by Fraile Press, based in London, UK.

Fred Carter published an excerpt of *Freedom & Prostitution* in a one-off strike solidarity publication, *Tender Hammers [Writing for the UCU Strike]*, in November–December 2019 in Edinburgh, Scotland. Many thanks for including the work.

Thank you to Joe Rathgeber at Radical Paper Press for turning part of *Freedom & Prostitution* into a beautiful broadside in January 2020.

An excerpt of *Freedom & Prostitution* appeared in *Homintern Magazine* in late February 2020, a big thanks to Alex Karsarvin for soliciting work, and to the rest of the editors there.

"THIS WORLD MUST DISAPPEAR: POSTSCRIPT FOR A FUTURE'S PAST," catalog essay for *Sapphire*, Weinberg/Newton Gallery, Chicago IL, Oct 7–Jan 14, 2017. Thank you to Nabiha Khan for commissioning this piece.

Portions of this manuscript where heavily influenced by or excerpts from *A Theory in Tears (ANNOTATIONS & CASES FOR FREEDOM & PROSTITUTION)* from Kenning Editions' Ordinance Series (2016), endless thanks to Patrick Durgin for publishing it and his patient support.

Parts of this work were derived from the performance *The Arm Collector*, by TRAUMA DOG (myself & Rachel Ellison) for the First Annual Festival of Poets Theater in Chicago, IL from December 2–5, 2015 at Sector 2337 curated by Patrick Durgin and Devin King.

Thank you to Judah Rubin for inviting me to read this work at the Poetry Project and publishing an excerpt on the website and newsletter in October 2015.

Thank you to Samuel Soloman, Natalie Cecire, Joe Luna, and Keston Sutherland for bringing me to the 10th Annual Sussex Poetry Festival in Brighton, UK, June 28-29, 2019 and to Dell Olson for having me read at the Royal Holloway Poetics Research Centre in London, UK, March 11, 2019.

Thank you to Azad Sharma for having me read at the Roebuck, London, UK, March 13, 2019 as part of the 87 Press Reading Series.

Thank you to Fred Carter and Dominic Hale for inviting me to read in Edinburgh, Scotland at their reading series, *JUST NOT*, on November 12, 2019.

The writing of this manuscript was made possible by generous support and residencies at the Headlands Center for the Arts in Sausalito, CA during Fall 2016 and ResidencyX at Flying Object in Hadley, MA during Summer 2014, organized and run by Guy Pettit and Karl Saffran. I have also completed work on this book thanks to research funding from my department at Linnaeus University in Kalmar, Sweden.

Profusive gratitude to my colleague and friend, Johan Ahlbäck, for his careful and nuanced design of this book, as it helped shape what it was and what it could become.

I am extremely grateful for the support and ferocious music of LINGUA IGNOTA (Kristin Hayter) whose liturgical power-violence opened up new voices for embodied survival and resilience, along with the many friends and comrades who have read this work or have been in conversation and given invaluable criticism, support, and inspiration at various stages: Brian Whitener, Nicole Trigg, David Buuck, James Payne, Rona Lorimer, Maya Andrea Gonzalez, Jami, Irene Silt, Jennifer Nelson, Ted Rees, Cody Troyan, Blake Butler, Anne Boyer, Jasper Bernes, Tom Allen, Fred Carter, Dominic Hale, Helen Pritchard, Helga Steppan, Thom Donovan, Fox Hysen, Amanda Trager and Eric Moskowitz.

Also by Cassandra Troyan
Throne Of Blood (Solar Luxuriance, 2013)
Blacken Me Blacken Me, Growled (Tiny Hardcore Press, 2014/Civil Coping Mechanisms, 2016)
Kill Manual (Artifice Books, 2014)

Photo by Fred Carter

Distributed by Small Press Distribution, Inc.
Printed in Canada

The Elephants Ltd.
www.theelephants.net

ISBN 978-1-988979-40-3 (print)

Book design by Johan Ahlbäck
Edited by Broc Rossell